"While attending the University of Hell I would want to major in John Barrios' *Here Comes the New Joy*—a class made up of intellect, inquiry, failure, heart, success, lyric triumphs, and human oddities. This is not a pass or fail class, but a place to wonder who we are, a place to light the exams on fire in hopes of a joy we have not yet learned about."

—Matthew Dickman, author of *Mayakovsky's Revolver* and Tin House Editor

"In this moving debut, the new joy isn't what we thought it was, but darker, more tough-minded. John Barrios stands in the fire and makes song of that work. The song is ongoing, altogether his own, 'unapologetically / alive / full.'"

—Paul Lisicky, author of *Famous Builder* and *Lawnboy*

"In finding his own unique and inspired voice, John Barrios has offered a gift to all of us, as he is showing us what it is to be a poet of our own psyche. Be forewarned, however, this book is contagious. After reading it, much to my surprise, as if getting a living transmission, I began writing poetry myself. Read this book at your own risk."

—Paul Levy, author of *Dispelling Wetiko: Breaking the Curse of Evil*

"*Here Comes the New Joy* unlocks a box of stories of what it means to know a life and all of its personal contradictions and curiosities. At times it is a conspicuous account of Past's shadowed memories, and other times it is a thick-woven description of Life's constants. In this welcome poetic page-turner, Barrios skips the flowers, and goes straight for the mud, splatter and all."

—Carrie Seitzinger, author of *Fall Ill Medicine*

This book published by University of Hell Press.
www.universityofhellpress.com

Cover Design by Vince Norris
www.norrisportfolio.com

Book Layout by Leah Noble Davidson

Published in the United States of America.
ISBN 978-1-938753-10-7

HERE COMES
THE NEW JOY

JOHN W BARRIOS

FOR HENRY

Acknowledgments:

I want to first thank Drew Swenhaugen, whose friendship in poetry is boundless.

I also want to thank Aaron Cohen, Michael Chase, Emily Kendall Frey, Matthew Dickman, Eve Connell, and Greg Gerding, for helping me, each in their own way, write this book.

TABLE OF CONTENTS

Joy

THE QUICK AND SICK OF LIFE.[1]

"We are in witchcraft, bedeviled."[2]

In March of 2012, I was diagnosed with depression. I knew things were not going well for a variety of reasons, but I still felt like myself. I started taking pills. I started on the "big pharma" and trusted in my therapists. At first I started to feel good again, almost great. A pendulum of feelings, swinging grief into joy into grief into joy, cutting me in half with every quick-swinging transition.

I often ask the Universe for help. I often ask the Universe for things. When I keep my eyes open, my heart open, these things are usually given to me.

A couch.

A table.

A pen.

Also the emotional. But those gifts are more difficult to see at first.

Pills.

"The cure, as much as the disease, appalls."[3]

A book.

I came across *Collected Poems, 1967* by Elizabeth Jennings on a dump cart at the bookstore where I work part-time. I usually grab any poetry, if it's essentially free, and open myself up to it. For the most part it is metered, Catholic-infused poetry I find little value in. But then came the poems on Jennings' mental illness. They sought me out—it took me a short time, but we eventually found each other. I can only say in rereading them "post" depression that what I valued in them came about during my own ride in the backseat.

"It does not seem a time for lucid rhyming;
Too much disturbs."[†]

I wonder if I would have been institutionalized had I lived in the late Fifties, or early Sixties. Most likely, due to the fact that I have a penis, I would not.

"So much is stagnant and yet nothing dies."[†]

Comfort. Nothing new for an essay. But then things shifted for me.

I stayed up all night almost every night for about two months. I used every Lego in the house and built a Babel Tower, floor to ceiling. My heart burst with pride. I couldn't wait to wake the boy from his slumber to see what Dad had accomplished. Two days later, I had no memory of building, or having a Lego Babel Tower.

I would soon have no memories.

I would soon forget what I was talking about mid-sentence. I learned how to casually pretend like I was distracted. Until I forgot why I was distracted and who I was with.

I was scared when I was lucid.

So we changed the channels on the television by changing my prescription.

Soon, I was planning a long walk from Portland, Oregon to Buffalo, New York. I calculated it would take two weeks. I had about twenty bucks and a favorite candy bar. I figured out my route in my head, as I've driven it many times in my years. I relived portions of the country from memory and imagined how exquisite they would be on foot. How joyful America would be to have me. I knew I had two days free to myself, yet two weeks seemed plausible.

My aches in these regards are minor in comparison to what Elizabeth Jennings experienced. But life is not about comparison. Comparison can poison the mind.

What truly scared me were the scenes in my head. Scenes I have had for years yet only on medication did I recognize as unhealthy.

When enraged, in depression, my mind would break the world into splinters. What takes three seconds in the real world feels like hours or a day in my mind. Pulling apart a house I am walking by. Shattering the windows; sharding the shards; splintering the wood with my fingernails. Burning in the fire just to feel a need to breathe. This imagery, this game while walking, eating ice cream, being mindless in a potentially joyful moment of life. The telephone pole in a heartbeat is ripped down and I am spiked fully with the splinters my hands have made of it.

I bleed and feel healed in the blood.

These are my true depressions.

"yet I still fight the stronger
Terror—oblivion—the needle thrusts in"[5]

I wore a beard for about six weeks. One day I woke up and looked in the mirror and wondered how in the hell I had grown a beard. I hate wearing beards. I can't stand seeing hair on my face in my peripheral vision. It's like dirt I can't wipe off my face. So I shaved. I sort of laughed it off. Then a couple days later, I reached up to feel my facial hair and it was gone. It was a shock to me. Where was my beard? I had forgotten I shaved it off. I had forgotten I had grown it. I had lost my sense of John.

This led me to the conclusion that "big pharma" was not working for me, but against me.

I am now clean of the pills. I am clean of the weed I once used to numb my mind of the pervasives. I am clean of the muddy relationships. I am not healed. I am not home. I am comforted by the idea of not being alone. Elizabeth Jennings came to me when I needed her. Her pain came to me when I needed it. Her words, like bullets down a rabbit hole, pierced my chest and spilled me out into the soft earth when I needed spilling.

This was going to be an essay.

This was going to be about Elizabeth Jennings' poetry of her mental health. I couldn't look at hers without acknowledging my own.

"I wish I knew
How I could help. But I have also been,
And am, your burden and your thread of pain."[6]

Poems Referenced

[1] Suicides (for a psychiatrist)
[2] Night Garden of the Asylum
[3] A Depression
[4] In a Mental Hospital Sitting Room
[5] Sequence in Hospital Part I Pain
[6] Suicides (for a psychiatrist)

HERE

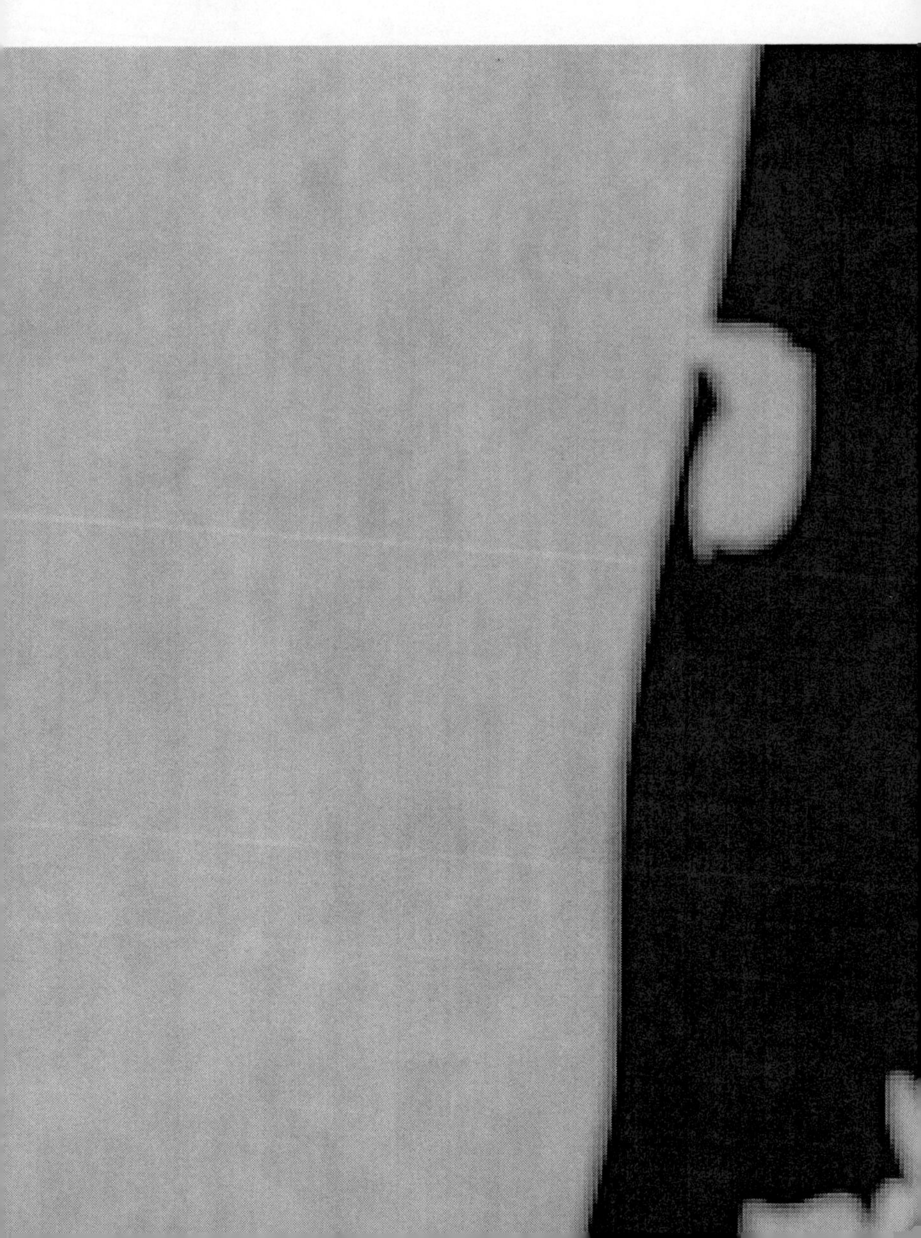

THE FIRST TIME I LIED

There were four
of us sitting in a circle
in Riverside Park. Tom was teaching
us younger boys how to properly eat
a slice of pizza. He said,
You can't just take a bite
at the apex of the slice, it's best
to fold it like a sandwich.
So that's what I was doing
when Michael sat between Dennis
and me. This small
act of self-inclusion
freaked Tom out. He stopped
eating. Michael was older
than Tom and he had a lot of acne. I knew
him only from sight and name.
He was a big player
in the T-Street Gang.
I stayed away from them
as best I could. I was
an outsider to their life. I was
new to the neighborhood and wasn't
welcome. My heart started beating

really fast and I was afraid
to eat the folded
slice I held in my hand.

He looked at me and said,

Mind if I eat that?

I went ahead and took as
big a bite as I could. I wanted
to look strong, tough, acceptable.
I felt stupid
when he laughed
at me. I looked at Tom,
as the pizza was his, and
he looked as scared as I felt.
I handed Michael the slice
and he did his thing.
He finally passed the nub end
of crust to his left
and asked me where I was from.
I told him
how our family sort of fled
and how we had a cousin who lived
here so that's how
we ended up here and all that.

He said he wanted the whole story.

I said,
My friend Tabitha and I
used to sit on the picnic
table in the backyard
listening to
mixtapes. We sat with the boom
box between us, passing small
talk back and forth.
We talked about nothing really. Mostly
just sat and watched the sky

and our breath. Our landscape
was power lines and chimneys on rooftops
with smoke rising here and there.

When we were called in for dinner
I grabbed the boom box and
she went to unplug it
from the socket on the outer
side of the house.
The cord just reached the table,
but when she grabbed it
to pull it from the socket,
she froze.
Her mittens were in
her pockets. She shook
uncontrollably. White foamed
at her lips and dripped
off her chin. Her eyes bulged.
She peed her pants.
Then she stopped and was perfectly still.
She stood slightly hunched,
the cord clenched in her
tiny fist.
Smoke rose from her head
and back. Her face
a bluish purple, she swayed
and then fell
over. I don't remember
freaking out.
I don't remember
screaming,
but I remember hearing screaming.
One scream.

One long continuous scream.
My mother raced into the yard
in her slippers, apron around her waist.
Her hand went to my mouth.

I said,
We moved here from Buffalo
the following spring. Folks
blamed us for her death. It went
to court and everything. It was ruled
an accidental death,
but my parents were held
liable
as it happened on their property.
My parents lost
their house and I had to leave
school early. I'll wait
until next year, after we get settled.
I'll be a year
older, but I don't mind.
I like it here.
I do
miss
the snow.

It was strange. It was like
we were the only two people sitting
in the park eating pizza.
Like the circle disappeared,
which it didn't, the others were just
quiet. Michael looked at Tom
with obvious discontent.

It started raining lightly
and I said, I have to get home. I
said it like a question and Michael
laughed at me again, but
this time in a friendly
manner. Not like we were pals,
but like we were
something.
I felt good about it.
I looked at his face.
He was 18 but looked 30.
He was pockmarked
heavily in his cheeks and had
yellow hair cut short.
His face looked like there was red
trying to ooze out
from the seams.

As it started to rain, he pulled
an umbrella from his backpack
and held it so we could both
walk under it. We walked
down T Street like this
passing others from his gang
who never spoke to him or looked
directly at him,
but they all looked at me.
After a few blocks
he asked more about Tabitha,
specifically, he wanted to know
how I felt
when I watched her die.
Nobody had asked me that before.

Not my mother.
Not the police.
Not my therapist.
Not her parents or my friends.
It was the one thing I wanted to talk about.
I didn't think it mattered what I felt.
She was dead. That's what
I told him.

I told him,
It doesn't matter what I felt, she was dead.
But you felt something? He replied.
Yea.
That's what I want to know.
I was scared.
No shit you were scared. I know that. How did you
feel?
Besides scared?
Besides scared.

I felt like the whole world had stopped.
The whole world stopped except the snow.
That's what I remember, besides
her face.

I remember my heart
was beating and it was snowing.
It was those big fat flakes
that drift in the air
real slow. Some landed
on her cheeks, on her nose
melting quickly. Her face
got red, real red

like she was a balloon.

I couldn't breathe. I didn't dare
try. No breath came
from her. She must've breathed in
one last time, 'cause once the power
went out, it went black,
the music stopped,
one long breath came out
of her, but it was like
it came out of all of her.
She was steaming.
The police said she was cooked,
fried. They said I was
screaming but I couldn't
hear it. Everything stopped.

All I saw was Tabitha's eyes
and I think she saw mine.

That's what I like to believe,
that we saw each other right
before she died.

So I guess I didn't really feel anything
in the moment. I mean, at the time,
everything was frozen
like the world around us, except
the snow falling and my heart
beating.

I didn't feel a thing.

He asked,
What was the song?
I live around the corner there.
I know where you live. What was the song?
It was Red
Rain by Peter Gabriel.

He looked at me.
It was like he was sizing me up.
Like he wasn't sure of what
I just said or he was taking it
all in real slow. Then he gestured
with his chin towards my house,
and said,
I ain't your papa,
kid, you can walk home
from here. I got some
things I gotta do.

With those parting words
he was gone.

Later that night
on the 11 o'clock
news I saw him
for the last time. He was
in the same clothes as when
we walked home.
He looked into the camera
from a small distance,
he didn't look scared one bit.
I know what he knows
and he knows I know it.

We both know
what it feels like to watch someone die.

Do you know him,
my mother asked,
he's from the neighborhood?

No,
I said,
I don't know him.

LIFE POEM

Will, I've got moths in my eyes

I am consumed by the madness of my
imagination

an old blues record pouring forth

foreign bone fragments used to rebuild the
bridge of my nose

pull open windows

finger roll to the right

sonorous, reflective parades

deception running through the room

Will, this is where I am:

under orange

sheets and a Star

Wars blanket

first snowfall

the phone rings

I know you.

Will, There is no work

but love

DOUBLE TAKE

information // waking body

window laces // bedroom

gorged eyes // treetops

playground // ground play

her dark pregnable self // silent interior

his fist in her heart
he looked he looked from walking away

THE MECHANIC,

PISTOL POLISHING

patience tended my garden
knees on the earth floor not the dance floor
or the porn shop
or the movie theater lit like

your bedroom
hot saliva

if I had wiped you clean with my
tongue heart eyes
it would still not have saved you
nor my garden

THE HISTORY ARCHITECT

twilight lanterns fragile light
a will to feel sown

swallow ash
plant a seed make the bed

the steam whistles warmth as she gathers her sword
the look of love eyes in-shined

as evening shifts we wonder
what we left back at the start

all the demons decided to cook for you
exposing heart's weakest moments

gathering nest
as something in the dirt rises towards you

clings to the sky
reaches high with direction

different sizes dragged across the floor
with answers chewing in their mouths

her eyes and her broken
flood become a hungry man's river
fishing out lavender ghosts
saddling the dragon knowing she was the one

soft gathering fool
her rock is filling up pages
canyons swollen in offered affections
secrets kept buried deep in the rift

never once smoked damages
torn the risk of a worthless heart
or refracted from the aching damn
the smallest parallels of wilderness

burn the old shame from the legacy
where bone begins its task
of waiting for the huntsman
the history architect

hands have never
given out forgiveness
smitten fields are man loved

sky grows to yawn
beds whisper birth

force passing
ears as breathless lobs

touch between sly paths
where ghosts have moored rain

flag on a broken arrow
adorns body's grief hill

THEY'LL FAIL YOU

Enough danger in the elements of leaving
Even when their fearless sigh goes away
Weathered walls, enameled pockets
Shadow following
Like a muted son
Laid out on the planks
Left over from the shipwreck
Leaning back in need
Breathing in the lichened air
Gentle earth, gentler still
When fearless sighs go away

DIOSCORIDES ON THE VIRTUES
OF COMMON JUNIPER

Out of the whimpering shadow
          slides skin of day
across pillars of grass. I read that
Common Juniper is one of the most
proliferous plants on the planet.
          It grows
in Asia
in Europe
in North America.

The Greek physician recommends applying
a poultice, or drink Juniper juice with wine
to fight the bite of a viper, struggling
with poisonous venom from the blood
working out the shadows.

ARSON HITS THE SPOT

just so she can
       sleep in-
       side fire

compared to most kids
we're really lucky
warm house
       un-
       building itself

A SPIDER IN EUCALYPTUS

spinning a beard of early November
light, reflection, voices
rising from a great distance

cacophonous

threat of cancer, harvest
thumb-smudged
photographs

FROM THE BRIGHT GREEN

"Rid your mouth of the sorrowing of the sparrows"
—Ana Bozicevic

a cross pollination
  a play in space
  sparkle splash
  winged shadows

dance: in a room of sawdust
  the falling of light is

  even if it happens too fast
  to feel flightless

rearrange oxygen
  intake valve is rusted
  brittle as a sparrow's heart

  quick beating
  blood about the fighting

  gone from a hungry mouth
  straw bed string fed

none of which is attached—muted! monsters
cluttering the sky, there could be 1 2 3 4 five
waiting
  for the next station, a layover
  flailing through the sky, that
  last short-beaked breath

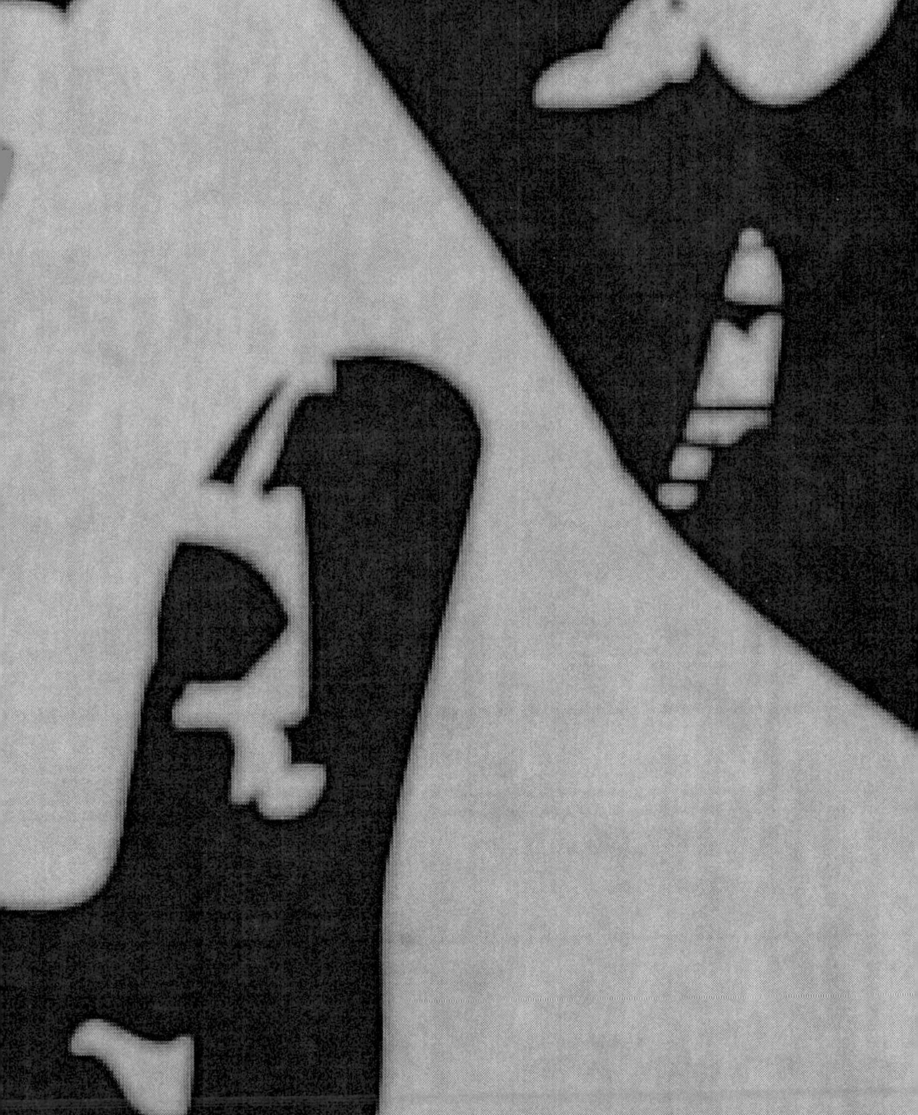

COMES

NEW MEXICO, 1970–SOMETHING

driving through rain on a new
mexico highway, midnight
1970-something, headlong into the white
lights of oncoming trucker traffic,
thought we'd be antlers above the mantle
in some home with whitewashed
pebbled lawn off the eastern side of this dead
highway. yet she swerved
and we spun, and she braked and we
swirled and then, somehow,
she held it tight and straight, before
releasing the brake, dovetailing us
into a muddy earth shoulder
while traffic continued like we were
not even there. eyes sparkling
off the rearview, into a wild
starless night, high-fiving
a near death on the cutting
room floor, edited from truckers
who never stopped to see
if we were okay, or alright, or
alive.

43 LINE TO THE SUNSET

The sunsets of frozen histories, caught in the floes
of today's bus ride up the Avenues. Whalebones
try to free breath the ocean of circumstance,
on past 19th, 20th, 21st, on past
Russian bakeries and Irish bars, the givers
and the takers, small carefully chosen fields
of deforestation, the long legs
of a white-wigged prostitute and her lawyer
lover, rubbing fingertips lacy stockings
as a panel of giggly Japanese girls in their matching
plaid skirts, polite mockeries
impending slaughter of self-reliance,
unlike the elder Vietnamese gentleman
whose tattoos claim triumph of life
after war. Stop after stop
the evening undresses its light
as a business woman smelling of lilacs
joins my seat, reading her dog-
eared Dostoyevsky she never got
around to in high school, engrossed,
eye-spotting her destination, my reading
over her shoulder, saying nothing of it,
when in fact I was inhaling her scents
fabric softener
tea tree shampoo
coffee
cigarettes
      I've passed my stop

EX LIBRIS: ALPHABET SOUP

[mountain puffing old man

   puff/sky/slide

[spider

spidery says, "I don't like
'papa
'I don't like
'snow
'I don't like
'swim
'I don't like
'skateboard
'I don't like
'like
'I love all
'things
'I don't like.

step in what makes sick
yea-yo stripe blue stripe

    [this is my red ball
    [still needing to throw

(old man puffing mountain

'I went underneath

'silly that game
'you do it please
'pleeease

[and once fox missed
  'I said almost
  'almooost

[I'm not all done

'come on come on

        this day eliminates *the*
        see it there, no __re
        see it

                (old puffing man mountain

     says,
'Hey, let's do a silly game
   'here's a book
   'here's a book
   'here's a book

[hey, come back here

        hide/out/side/outside

[no bodies there
   no, I don't like
   her,
   no, I don't like
   her, no bodies __re

⸢I really want outside
⸢peaches

open
open
open
open

I want to show you

come out
come out
come out

I need to spell

⸢like a half circle, the C
⸢flag upon mountain, the P

(did he know that?
(did it matter?

Mountain knew 'releefe'
we spell 'relief'

elec   tric
soft lines   __re
and   __re
and   __re

(I lock it
but words are freedom
(oh, the lock!

words are water, but
        (I can't get inside
are fire, words
        (goodbye goodbye goodbye goodbye
air,

    [can we go out?

come and get me

(that wilting flower, the e

this is a music he makes
a man, a mountain, a puff

(reaching for rain, the Y

        [in the spring
        [in the Spring

            (did he write to erase?
            (did he erase to write?

'Can't catch me!

(that fishing line, the g

        (see
        (see
        (see

red(riots
blue(beasts

green(ghosts
white(whispers
brown(bringeth
          —AGAPE!

"I said, 'air

'air

          [a tap
          [a dance
          [pencil pencil
          'scratch 'scratch

junk mail makes best friend
mountain sees to that
puffing slide sky

(that pyramid of hope, the A
(that child at play, the a

this is landscape

     (boy screams
     (boy laughs
          [possession

landscape is this

     (sand laughter
     (his   his

          [sandness

[nessness

so] out of libraries
like] ducks tail-sweeping ponds
do] alphabets erase themselves
as] voices raised go muff-
led] an open book
on] a smoke
to] feel fluttering hands howl-
ing] words fly

(destination

[childhood minuets
[cadaverous minestrone

alphabet soup

eat)en page by page
eat)en spoon by spoonful
eat)en library by library
eat)en unsatisfied z

[mountain puffed old man
(chewing words through drink

'air

WE DUG THE EARTH TO HOLD OUR BONES

Soon we had lunch // politics of sheepish
graves // to actually touch // vulgar lunar
(sometimes that's what a friend is for // radiant
photographs) summer wheezing around cocktails
// unidentifiable // great lives chained // huddled
a combination // middle dream middle name // to
imagine him // mirror double indulgence // cup
drink dregs
    strange month
standing two hours without throngs of lively
conversation //
among other things // vulnerability
strength // character
    unflinching   game
    streeting   visionary
    cynical   contemporary
    river   safe
        I've forgotten that night
        sleeping happy nothing
        sheepish graves

people still eat words scraping along the edge of
the plate

NAUSEA ROSE

Three bites of the fruit
Banana splayed open
Limp tripod
Waiting

An elder off the tier of landscape
An artifact
In a house of her own markings
A mezzanine of empty mouths

To disappear in Shanghai
She sighed

A love bird, a get-me-through-my-day,
A native to my kin
Of folk who fear their name

Wood slats blind neighbor's expressionless view

    A bed has faith in itself
    Soft spot eyes

    White as kill
The contents of a bottle

    A kiss
    Winter in a day with the lion's paw

    On the horizon
    The great mist of notation

SUMMER, 1986

That sort of haunting
I was thinking about

   (streets unlit
   (dimly shadowed

That darkness seeps
out the stereo

   (speakers
   (speaking

No toll at this age
Nothing to tell/sell

   (memory latch come loose
   (latch loose memory come

1
sidewalks
different dirt,
black where blood
white where bleached
pink where gummed
  (and she gummed (but later

2
then feet
(*Oh how many, many feet we meet!*

shoes describes wordlessly
color, cleanliness, dividing posts of youth
damn feral minds (absentee

3
Shopping list of cool:

> (place here ________ whatever
> made you cool or the absence
> of which made you uncool of
> which un/cool/ness made you
> cool to the cool/less, who
> were cool (cool is a word
> you never want gushing again

Number 1—girlfriends
(there are no other numbers without number one.

4

standing on a large chunk of concrete just so our
mouths were aligned for kissing.

5

Riverwalk. Riversmell. Riverride. Riverfight. Riverfish. Riverrage. Riverboner. Riverrape. Riverpower. Riverbugs. Rivergangs. Riverhate. Riversport. Riversilence. Riverdistance. Riverdarkness. Rivermusic. Riverburgers. Riversit. Riverschool. Rivermove. Riverrock. Riveralone. Riverhorse. Riverbait. Riverliver. Riverbed. Riverquiver. RiverOhRiver. Riverscape. Rivermind. Riverescape. Rivergate. Riversplendor. Riverasis. Rivernecklace. Riverboat. Riverbottom. Riverheart. Riverreader. Riverrocket. Rivercocksuck. Riverpine. Riverwinter. Riverwater. Riverrun. Riveralliteration. Rivercool. Riverraiders. Rivertramp. Riverover. Riverlover. Riverriver. Rivercycle. Riverside.

6
take the gangly boy by the shoulder
under umbrella
and stroll down Danger Street

    (every pair
    (of eyes
    (sees you
    (sees him
    (us together
    (fear lifts

        I've got to meet a friend behind the high school
        he says
        he says
        You're okay

7
he was on the news for murder hours after he
walked me home
gang leader blues

8
his steel eyes inside my fear
cleansing it

9

seeyouseemeseemefuckitall
seeyouseemeseemefuckitall

10
still chasing fear some
thing new found residence in there
his pocked face watches
over this new fear
over me
(______

11
because I came so fast
with your tongue in my mouth
your huge squishy breasts spinning in my palms
your hot thigh rubbing my hardness
(moaning(breathing(eyeless
dry humping adolescence

12
how great we felt and would never feel again
together

13

would I recognize the menstrual cycle of the
    sidewalk
by the way she dotted her "i"s before making the
    body of the letter,
by pulling mud-puppies from the shallows of the
    river
and hiding them in the trunk of her father's blue
    Cadillac,
by stealing weed from her uncle's closet,
blow jobs on night porches,
headbangers banging heads on stop signs,
(so many aimless leather jackets
by the amount of stolen beer?
would the cycle recognize me?

14
I'm going to eat Doritos and pretend
I never lost my virginity and am 15 and am
afraid and am free in that tormented innocence.

15
did I walk away or run? funny how
I moved yet never really left. Never
grew out of the wonder. Age doesn't ans(her
questions; I)t blurs.

A VICTORIAN HOME ON

THE OREGON COAST

She is calling out
While I wait for mine
I see a thousand spines on wooden shelves
Have I not conducted my syllables to the orchestra?

A thousand selves brush together in opposing
  mirrors
Mourning helps
Leaves gather around the windowsill auditioning
Spiraling and floating

Dying moths are put on stretchers made of clay
Autumn is pulled off the battlefield
The moon descends upon my mouth
It is done

No trace of the latticework
Where water is sewn to sky
If only one had the mind to tug
Ever so gently along the horizon

Our two cats bicker away like rain
Against the window. One cat with wild eyes
The other in love with my neck
The smell and salty taste of me

Blackening blue envelops the receding
Neighborhoods, sometimes a bridge
I put a white candle in
The tin lamp I pulled from the fire

Fleas have invaded
Pinch them with fingernails
Chemical warfare
Drown them in hot saliva

The bone chip floated between skull and skin
Brain fluid seeped through the hole in her skull
Doctors were more concerned with what might find
  its way in
Rather than what might have escaped

\---

Moon glided
Across the surface of my body
In bath water
Through an open window

\---

Erica cries behind hand-waving, smiles
A lock of her hair arrives at Heaven's door
No one is there to receive it
I think Heaven's Postmaster is playing a wicked game

\---

Vincent bartering river-rat words
Drooling brick alley roads
Camouflaging French-eyed whores
A biography of abuse, absence

\---

Pouring milk into a bowl of cherries
While listening to Beethoven's *Moonlight
Sonata*, something so lovely, so desolate
A Victorian home on the Oregon Coast

What surprises the eye is repetition to the heart
No matter. Moments swell
A blinding focus, unspoken
Hesitation at the elevator door

Are we not the definition of incalculable space?
Each jointed question a trapped temper
Even now as I hammer this down
It cannot be undone

There are certain moments of clarity
Along the footpath ...
            Was it really
A thousand ships?

BRUISED BEGINNINGS

Our little group
Hiding under gymnasium stairs
Pulling ghosts from cardboard
Pouting plastic eyes
Circling a direction of nowhere
Calling spirits for answers.

It is all fake and yet
How would my friends know her middle
Name was Rose.

Or that she never met my little brother
Or cared much for my father
Or that she called me Little Hickey
Due to bruising on my face
From a difficult birth

THE RED NOTEBOOK

my ghost tells me to steal it
an alphabet left in the backseat
while the author runs in to buy cigarettes and beer

just take it, he says, *feel its heft*

my ghost gets me into a lot of trouble
introduces a lot of bad decisions

the window is open, he says, *there you go*

I barely feel it, it feels
so perfect, cradled

don't even look at the title, he says, *just torch the fucker*

I read it instead
he says my logic is flawed

FROM THE FRONT SEAT
OF THIS HEARSE

I remember sitting on the couch
watching TV, but
I don't remember
the couch. My mom
liked to lay
on the floor
in front of the TV.
The house smelled
of cabbage soup. I hated
her hair, and my aunt's
hair! She stayed
with us one
summer and the two
of them lay
on the floor
with their feathery
hair farting
cabbage soup
in front of the TV while
my poor stepfather
and I gagged
trying to watch
Batman reruns.
It was our only
fun time together
my stepfather and I

watching reruns
from when
he was
a boy. I
once told him
I could be
Robin
to his Batman. He
ignored me. I knew
he wanted me
to want to
be Batman.

SLIPPAGE

After so many
years, this
picture of you
on the Internet
reminds me
how small and geeky
we once were.
Even at this
later stage
in our lives, there
you are, still
this dreamy lanky
girl with an over-
sized mouth
laughing toothy ideas
joyful moment
which never
seems to end or
last. Funny
how timelessness
works,
never truly
committing.

NOW WHAT

        to the reader
        an illegible pact

internal ink patterns pushing a
scrolling disadvantage

between the sheets

What for of the as she whispered

            As what of the for I smothered

What for the as of she mustered

sunk down in bubble-battled wind
pop pop pop pop

a rhythmic
force scattering pomegranates

tumbling morning
breath inside a vacuous kiss

leaves bartering tree swords
for fluttered flight

sun shards declassifying floorboards
across an arch of mid-day
    vineyards steeped in music produces

chronicles of Latin transcript
with every sip

NEW

RECOGNITION

The accolades and fubar girls
The roasts and the duck hunt
The wild detritus
That adds up

Soaking one-word columns under sentence headers
Have faith in a handshake with a Panda
Express employee who tried to slip you
Pickled ginger between your fingers

It was certainly an abstract objectification
In most cases we would simply lay out the details
Highlight the lows with a swiveling voice
Show off the highs with dancing hand gestures

THE CYCLOPS

By the bottling company, behind where trains
track the outer ear of our little town, a snowman
with one eye watches the crows
crowd the dead body, gorging
steaming air
        she told me she would
never act like a panther leaping from a tree
yet we went out between the mansions
blood spilled, dripping through parking
lots and Subway Express bathrooms, greeting
the sunrise with one eye.

INK BARK

After you left to go for a walk in the real woods, I sat at the computer where you left your Word document open. I hit the End button and started typing from there, from the end, and an hour went hazily by in this little room while you, out there in the big room, had no idea how time was for me, as I had no idea how time was for you, perhaps the hour whittled away in small succulent strokes, or maybe ten footfalls felt like a minute trapped in a snow-filled hourglass as swallows scuttled in lower branches off the path, knocking out last year's nest to make room for this year's, where babies will pull worms from beaks, where feathers will molten, wings expand as air tightens and loosens at once as sky lifts, earth falls and little feet get tucked up into the belly until claws need to reach out for a branch.

PATCH OF VALLEY

View from your kitchen window
Fading fog pink
Landscape of hills
Morning sky blue
The Pacific Ocean
Dances with the clank of the radiator
And survives

One night while I rolled my tongue across your
belly you
              told me exactly how you felt in Spanish.
              I retaliated in my broken
French. In November I'll be somewhere.
Place a moment on the finger.

Cold rises linoleum bare feet calves
Water in your bathroom running
Toilet flushes
Waiting for coffee
Running water in the bathroom stops
A cabinet is closed
A door opens
Your fresh morning face
Responsibility, or a crowned child

The apple shape two bodies make.
Yosemite Valley, the memory
of an afghan. A mother's
making, not smiling. Dawn
saying *you should look more like your father.*

In this corridor smell
of this bed
yours. Repeating glass, repeating
glass bed. Where moths sleep
                    under eyes.

Falling towards death, not calm
pull splinters raw cheek

sun over El Capitan, cool
breeze whittles out

a patch of valley

Kiss. Kiss.
Photograph.
Head tilted slightly towards.

I thought I might
cry if I didn't
something soon

border of the chamber
blind man in the kitchen
pot of coffee

lifted the whole
just to look
at a hula girl painted
inside of the bowl

Daydreaming the *Bull*

I breathed in

you
        fell asleep

hollowed out march a darkness
storm and ancient humming

        below a haloed earth

to sleep in the glacier of ease
that lonely moment of there

        when I can't see I will know

I am home

THE POET AT THE PODIUM

Somehow we date
      I get to taste her breath after long
      evenings outside
      I get to finger her nipples and tongue her
      lower back
      after all, sex is gorgeously sleeping
      beneath our sheets

Somehow she is able to make me cry
      makes her want me more
      somehow intellectually

Somehow what I don't do is what gets her excited
      what I do is really
      hurting me is exciting
      she says that she just doesn't like anything
      somehow or anybody

Somehow I am an exception
      love is never spoken
      she reads dreams as poetry and poetry as
      sheep
      we baaaa at all the right moments
      the audience feels as I do in the sheets
      this auditorium in this dusty college town
      diving down

Somehow on this spinning from her alphabet galaxy
        I don't breathe until she allows it
        I like it like this

Somehow she even struggles out a smile
        all that curly red barbed wire hair
        snaking my halo-sluicing brain
        tissue audible from the podium

INTERNET HAIRCUT

I forgot I was ever in love with you and your book
  arrived
I was cut in half. I was cut in half
By the splinters from your bone
Your blue eyes are colder than the photograph can
  say
Lines around your mouth a little deeper
I eat your painted mouth
The desire to stain is different from the staining
I eat your razor wire hair
In many haircuts I can hear you
Reading bleached wood
Building language from the blood
About the wolf's mouth
It cuts

AWAKENING

the heart that breaks the bone
rebuilds
the body with an eventide of blood

archaic in ritual

chestnuts in the kitchen split and cooling
whisper a child's name

AND MERRY LAY AMONG
THEM, BUSTED

heading south dripping
midriff glances in that French-eyed way of hers

such heavy breathing, such highlights

vision flashes
hands bleeding, burning, feeling good
pulling telephone pole splinter by splinter

    fingers, nails
    gory glory
            euphoria
    quick breath
    breathless

                        houses
                        torn apart

hands daggers that bleed
muscular
cactus

torn, not torn
ordering food cart foodness
bleeding blood cart bloodness
scattering
mind tumbles
a clot

in the marrow, a clot
in the home
homeless, now a child
now a spent penny crusted
scraped
pocketed and forgotten

sailed upon, so still this
manic, wind
storms, harvested, waves
of saliva and tears
a landfill

   like always
   letting go
   train upon the tracks crawl
   faster than the last
   look upon
   soft cheeks

dance, not dance
hands, not hands
blood, not blood
fear, not fear
manic, not manic
pills, not thrills
hands, not holding
holding, not hands

   look upon that tent pole
   look upon splinters
   fear not the fool
   foolish may be

hands carved dance of mind
flushed
forgotten, not forgiven

YES AND YES

writing, difficult, manic episode poem, she wanted to *push me* for more on this one, and I think that it is good, but I'm crying, and sometimes the hurt, the pain, the remembering of tragedy so succulent in the mind, so near, so fresh and still, painful and tumbling and every ounce reminds you of how you once were and how far you have come and how far you have to go and how much the pain in the brain is a fire with pills like gasoline, good to get it out good to say good riddance good just to be sometimes, because sometimes, just to be is all you have.

HERE COMES THE NEW JOY

It's okay
you can blame the flood on me
if that makes your spendthrift
wallet palatable for those fancy boots
all tied up to the knees, unworn
in the back of your closet
next to one of those
misplaced truths, hidden
like a song on shuffle
desperate for its turn to rage
a beat
to fight for grace inside this scratching
pen, figure skating
on paper, a littered floor,
no more noticeable than absence
on a sofa stirring coffee with a down feather,
while sparks in the chimney,
ash in the lungs, a sacrament,
a porcupine ascending
landscape, a mountain,
its thorny pride pricking
unapologetically
alive
full

REALIZING GHOSTS

erased by child
exhausted
sun wet
spots on shirt
map your
play
squirrel inside
      laughing
      growling
      growling

THE STUFFED VERSION

OF HIMSELF

When James came
across it, she talked
of her childhood,
of his child-
hood, actually.
"Your best friends, I fucked them all.
Well, not all of them, but most of them,"
she winked, giggled,
hushed,
"I blew the rest."

How strange
she was,
how familiar.

"But
when I got pregnant I knew
exactly who
the father was."

James
went
pale.

"This isn't your life,"
she said. "The one
I've been living." Here

her tone changed,
"There's a great stuffed version of your life
out there.
I met her once.
Such a sweetheart."

He had to sit
down, as he did
he saw it, a malformed
balloon
made from all the raw
sex she, *or he,*
had
with all of his friends,
growing inside of her.

"Do you want to touch my belly?
Your belly?"

"I'm going to
throw up."

"It's the pregnancy,"
she said, "you're sort of
feeling it all
at once."

She reached down
took James'
hand
placed it
on her belly, *his* belly,
the warmth of it,
the tightness,

and the movement inside.
"Do you know what you're having?" he asked
meekly, his mouth dry.

She just laughed.
She laughed so loud.

"Here, you can feel all four
paws if you work your way around."

James wanted to pull his hand away, but he couldn't.
It was like a magnet that belly, *his* belly.

It took about twenty minutes and it was done.
James stood in a bloody fecal mess
wiping afterbirth from his Jackalope love child.

He hardly noticed she was gone.

James held his little Jackalope
nursed him from his own breast.

"You are the ultimate expression
of the opposite of everything
I ever was or ever will be
and I love you."

He never felt more alive.
Hold your hand, I would, I would but
closeness is not what I long for with you,
only with you I long
for the distance. Fading
beyond perimeter of a star-

ry eastern night, that place opposite of
where I craved nipple, of
separation, which helped me walk up
the long blade of forgiveness

Was it I?

Mathematicians add up a day with a firework
display of minutes—gloriously magnified
minutes—in
summer night skies—
just—I let go

of your hand to feel the cool grass, wind-
blown, an illusion
—of regret, of regret
of letting go

MANY PEOPLE FROM

VARIED WALKS

relative to what
my time here in silence
even when the screaming peaks
                              silence
something mortal to the touch
touching itself, even
                    the idea of the slightest
physical truth, closing in, enveloping
one substance for another
                              flesh to rock
rock to grass, grass to dirt, dirt
to root and so on and, well,
it's all relative to something

        the idea of the slightest

                the idea of the slightest

9:55 P.M.

Mid-summer. The neighbor's Westies rattle
the moon with their evening tongues, scaring off
the last of the stars I was saving for my dreams.
I'm hunting Autumn
colors at dusk, light
waxing red dust
parachuting passage into night

THE CRADLE OF HIS ARMS

He never taught me
how to hammer a nail, play
piano, pick-up lines, love.
There is a song he played,
none of the "survived by"
people have heard him play
it. Only Richard. It may be
a requiem for his mother or
a salsa for his saucy wife;
a simple solo for his
not-so-simple sister, perhaps;
"an old cracked tune" for his father,
a man he never mentioned
in my company. I like to believe
his song is for me, a ballad,
a lullaby for an infant aged 25.
I would crawl into the cradle of his arms
and he would stroke my head and back
with his musical fingers playing
his lost song on the keyboard of my spine,
humming, lulling me to sleep.
       Now
here I am, Richard, at your death-
bed pressing my song along your arms,
whispering my mother's name
into your ear, lips to your
leathery, yellowy skin. *Shhh.*
Only we can hear, Richard,
you and I.

THE STILLING

She slipped
out
the back
door,
through
silver edges
of salty
time,
into a corridor
of white upon white.
Breathing
is not
necessary.
Massaging
her frozen
legs
will not
keep the
blood
from
stilling.

WINTER VIOLETS

New poems in the vault
chance and circumstance.

New languages whispering up
from the frozen yard, fresh
off the heels
of the dog's evening run.

I touch a place in the sky
half expecting to find memory.

I shake the cold and wipe
the dog's paws in the back hall
of my father's house,
now my home.

THREATS

In great distances
cacophonies are almost silent.

What is the protocol of silence?

After my own harvest
I shall rise as from an altar.

I can smell eucalyptus
from that same distance.

BOILING PHALLUS

My mother boils an ear
of corn. Her clitoris groans.

On the second shelf, behind
a stack of plates, a stack of bills.

Husband never married,
lover limp outside her door.

Passion from her breast, dried
milk. No more water. No blood.

Collectors come, molesters
go. She stands alone boiling

an ear of corn, her clitoris
silently groans.

IT IS IN

A violent glow
 surrounding us
yellow sheen
 light summoning

up the orgasm
 creation
burrowing roots
 reaching a sky
we surrender

 to pulse
in the moist
 throat of awakening
magnified
 eyes of eyes
leaves
 feathering out

dawn's rising
 unfolding
azure quickness
 between
shadow and light.

GATHERING

In the shadow of rocks
current whisper smoothly
across scales.

Safe in the dark
not cold.

Fisherman
has lifted his pole out
of the high grass
baiting leeches
blood worms.

Sundried seagulls on a beach,
breeze pimpling.

In the kitchen
rinsing out the innards
under cold water
feeling scales slip
through a dream of rocks,
of shade, of fishermen rustling
offshore, gathering
poles and bait.

When we finally
slept, I felt the weight
of the act bobbing
in my dreams
like lures on a line.

SHADOW

I saw a guy on the bus who looked and behaved like
  me.

It was like I was a ghost watching the machine of
  my life.

Elusive buoyancy, floating, surviving.

To hear your sonorous voice untangling words
  from my grip.

It's what settles in the shallow foggy morning.

THE POOL CLEANER

Gordon was cleaning his pool.
First he let out all the water. He did this
by putting one end of the hose in the water and
sucking out of the other until water flowed
from his pool through the hose into the bushes.
Then he climbed into the pool and washed the walls
the floor
with a scrub brush and plenty of soap. He rinsed it
all down the drain.
The next day he repeated the process.

What are you going to do now? asked his wife the next
evening.
I'm not sure.
It sure looks clean.
Yeah.
*I haven't seen it look that clean since we first had it put
in.*
I know. It's clean.

Gordon walked out the back patio and looked up to
the sky.
It was pale, full of clouds.
No stars.
Crickets and the swallowing of beer
the sounds of night. His wife doing the dishes.
After, she smoked with him.

I spoke with Larry this afternoon.
He said he wants to buy Linda's car.

He can use it for his daughter.

She took a long drag off her cigarette before
continuing.

I told him I had to talk to you about it first.
What do you think?

Gordon finished his last gulp of beer and said,
That sounds like a good idea. If his daughter needs
the car, then I think it's a very good idea.

He opened another beer from his six pack.
She snubbed out her butt.
You should come in soon, it's going to rain tonight.
I'll be in later, he said,
I want to watch.

He heard the television come on inside and knew it
would be on all night.
He watched the rain.

In the morning the pool was half full again
with the previous night's rain. He got the hose
and drained it before breakfast.
The people who installed
the pool were coming that afternoon to fill it
with dirt. He planned on a vegetable garden.

He sat in Linda's car while the pool was being filled,
weeping as he watched.

SOLITUDE FOR LOVERS

rolling the resolve
refusing suits
same path, different door

growing
like milkweed between train tracks

sandalwood

falling through graces
silver glazed, threaded

dreaming of children running
she says she can't depend on cycles
anymore

no patience
I say

rain pissing down

the back of her head shrinking up
the sidewalk

THE GLOW

there is no authenticity
to how near you are

cherry blossoms pink
halo neighborhood
brief sacrifice light
in a cloud
riding a bike
understanding
nothing
but the need for shelter

if my heart were a house
it would be on fire

IN A BOAT WITH THIS LIGHT

how delicate
her hands

unbraiding
hair

I'm haunted

kisses not enough

                    bird
she's lonely
                    zipped
filed away

MONOLOGUE OF THE DYING

You're the first
person I'm coming to see
because you are the farthest point
from where I am going

I'm leaving, John,
I'm leaving unused
telephone books, shiny keys,
a blinking answering
machine, an unmade bed,
dishes in the sink, the dog
unleashed in the yard,
my children in other people's
houses, the cap from the toothpaste
on the counter, laundry in the wash,
milk in the fridge, bread
toasting in the toaster,
your mother
on hold, her pantyhose
in the neighbor's shrubbery,
a cigarette burning
by the bed,
the liquor cabinet empty,
this page undated, the rent
check late, the gas
tank on E, the lights
on, and especially, John,
I'm leaving you.

GOALS

write novel
write poems
teach children
fall in love
play music
> help keep house clean
> help with the cat
> talk to Melissa more

pray to god she destroys all computers

find solace in simplicity
find a dream and live it

> find a new job!

let the hard blue sky fall right through me
sad young cardinals are trying to sing
i should not be allowed to touch anything

MID-CENTURY MODERN

wedding present star clock
has never kept time, belongs
to an art of its own

evolved additions
rotations
civilized frieze

a house and a stomping

magazine subscriptions
feeding the grind

tv series unfinished
books unread
a mezzanine of empty glasses
an elder off the tier

inner landscapes

wood slats blind morning
light, something whispered

oh

gold, cold, letting go

eyes white as kill
giving way to the missing
of her shuffling through rooms

brittle spine, wiggling toes
wearing just the right sweater

breathing in the blooming dogwoods
a thousand wasted years

a bed without a body
never naked, never built
a spoonful of kisses
a horizon of notation

I've been hard, but I've been true

JOY

"Sorrow prepares you for joy. It violently sweeps everything out of your house, so that new joy can find space to enter. It shakes the yellow leaves from the bough of your heart, so that fresh green leaves can grow in their place. It pulls up the rotten roots, so that new roots hidden beneath have room to grow. Whatever sorrow shakes from your heart, far better things will take their place."

—Rumi

NOTES:

Some of the works have previously appeared in the same or different forms. In *Nailed Magazine*, The Quick and Sick of Life; *Small Doggies Magazine*, Summer, 1986; *Unshod Quills*, The History Architect; *Stealing Time*, Awakening; *Kin*, A Spider in Eucalyptus; *Housefire*, ex libris, We dug the earth to bury our bones, From The Front Seat of This Hearse, Recognition (aka We had no paper to write it down so we just said it again and again...), The Stuffed Version of Himself; *2GQ (aka Plazm)* The Pool Cleaner; *Daddy Cool, an Anthology of writing by Fathers*, The First Time I Lied; *Gathering of Leaves, an Anthology of writing by Booksellers*, The Cradle of His Arms.

Elizabeth Jennings poetry taken from *Collected Poems, 1967*, Macmillan and Company.

"and merry lay among them, busted" taken from Charles Olson's *Maximus Poems* 11.16.

John W Barrios is a poet, sometime essayist, and full-time father living in Portland, Oregon.

THIS BOOK IS ONE OF THE
MANY AVAILABLE FROM
UNIVERSITY OF HELL PRESS.
DO YOU HAVE THEM ALL?

by Tyler Atwood
an electric sheep jumps to greener pasture

by Eirean Bradley
the I in team
the little big book of go kill yourself

by Calvero
someday i'm going to marry Katy Perry
i want love so great it makes nicholas sparks cream in his pants

by Leah Noble Davidson
Poetic Scientifica

by Rory Douglas
The Most Fun You'll Have at a Cage Fight

by Brian S. Ellis
American Dust Revisited

by Greg Gerding
The Burning Album of Lame
Venue Voyeurisms: Bars of San Diego
Loser Makes Good: Selected Poems 1994
Piss Artist: Selected Poems 1995-1999
The Idiot Parade: Selected Poems 2000-2005

by Joseph Edwin Haeger
Learn to Swim

by Lindsey Kugler
HERE.

by Johnny No Bueno
We Were Warriors

by Stephen M. Park
High & Dry

by Michael N. Thompson
A Murder of Crows

UNIVERSITY OF HELL PRESS

universityofhellpress.com

CPSIA information can be obtained at www.ICGtesting.com
Printed in the USA
BVOW02s1918120814

362630BV00002B/12/P